FIVE THINGS
EVERY CHRISTIAN
NEEDS TO GROW

R. C. SPROUL

W PUBLISHING GROUP™

www.wpublishinggroup.com

A Division of Thomas Nelson, Inc.
www.ThomasNelson.com

To Archie Parrish, for his utter
devotion to Kingdom Focused Prayer

Published by W Publishing Group, a Division of Thomas Nelson, Inc.,
P.O. Box 141000, Nashville, Tennessee, 37214.

Scripture quotations are from The
New King James Version, copyright © 1979, 1980, 1982,
Thomas Nelson, Inc., Publishers.

Library of Congress Cataloging-in-Publication Data

Sproul, R. C. (Robert Charles), 1939-
Five things every Christian needs to grow / by R.C. Sproul.
    p. cm.
ISBN 0-8499-1754-9
1. Christian life--Reformed authors. I. Title.
BV4501.3 .S665 2002
248.4—dc21   2002005654

Printed in the United States of America
05 WOR 9 8 7 6 5 4

CONTENTS

Introduction ⁕ v

Chapter 1
BIBLE STUDY ⁕ 1

Chapter 2
PRAYER ⁕ 22

Chapter 3
WORSHIP ⁕ 41

Chapter 4
SERVICE ⁕ 55

Chapter 5
STEWARDSHIP ⁕ 73

INTRODUCTION

It's a worldwide phenomenon. Every four years the world pauses and holds its collective breath while the Olympic games take place. Staggered so they occur two years apart, the summer and winter games feature the finest athletes in the world competing in well-known sports such as running, skiing, basketball, and gymnastics, as well as comparatively unknown events such as curling and the triple jump. The athletes come from virtually every nation on the face of the earth, a vast, magnificent display of humanity in all our diversity: different skin colors, different languages, different dress styles, different lifestyles.

These national representatives have much in common as they enter the stadium and gather under the Olympic banner with its five interlocking rings representing unity among the nations of Africa, the Americas, Asia, Australia, and Europe. They all stand there, together, and take the Olympic oath, pledging to uphold the highest ideals of sportsmanship. They all strive to attain that Olympic ideal: *Citius, Altius, Fortius* (Swifter, Higher, Stronger). And they all put their years of training and preparation to the utmost test, head to head against their fellow competitors.

Being a Christian is not an acquired skill or discipline like diving or ice-skating. It is a living, vital relationship with the God of the universe, a relationship that begins when a person becomes a new creation in Him and receives Jesus as Lord by faith. But, like Olympic athletes, Christians are called upon to train, to make sacrifices, to embrace certain disciplines in order to give God "our utmost for His highest." This book deals with five of those disciplines: (1) Bible study, (2) prayer, (3) worship, (4) service, and (5) steward-ship. Like the interlocking rings of the Olympic flag, these five practices raise a standard of ideals for Christians from every nation and people group. Just as the athletes work hard to achieve their best performances, our diligence in attending to these aspects of the Christian life will help determine our effectiveness in serving our Lord.

Olympians sweat and sacrifice for years and sometimes

decades for the chance to compete and, hopefully, win a medal and hear the applause of fans the world over. This stands as a once-in-a-lifetime experience for a select few gifted and dedicated men and women. God's people likely will not receive the world's adulation, but we will someday hear the words, "Well done, good and faithful servant."

Do you not know that those who run in a race all run, but one receives the prize? Run in such a way that you may obtain it. And everyone who competes for the prize is temperate in all things. Now they do it to obtain a perishable crown, but we for an imperishable crown. (1 Corinthians 9:24–25)

Enjoy your race!

1

BIBLE STUDY

The man writhed in excruciating agony. The pain he felt was not physical. He wished it were; he had dealt with that kind of pain before, and knew he could find relief by balms or even a drunken stupor. This pain required something greater . . . much greater for its cure. This was a spiritual agony, a darkness of the soul where one felt suspended by a fragile filament over the gaping jaws of hell.

The pain was the shame, devastation, and ruin of personal humiliation, the public exposure of secret sin. This man was a hero, a national celebrity, a noted warrior, statesman, poet, musician, and spiritual leader. During his lifetime he was the object of popular songs that celebrated his exploits. He catapulted to national fame when he championed his people by killing his army's most feared enemy, a monstrous titan, with simply a sling and one smooth stone. He was a loyal subject of his king, even when that man sought to kill him.

The man was David, the second king of Israel. His reign ushered in the golden age of Israel as he extended the boundaries of the nation to unprecedented lengths. Under his leadership this tiny country, about the size of the state of Maryland, became a major world power. Situated on the land bridge that connects Africa with Asia and Europe— through which ran international trade routes—Israel was positioned in a place of strategic geopolitical importance.

David's greatness went beyond politics and culture. He is best known for being a spiritual leader, a man after God's own heart. When he fell into monstrous sin, it was a calamity not only for David and his family, but also for the entire nation. Despite his spiritual strength, he was so blinded to the evil in his own heart that it took a direct confrontation by the prophet Nathan to awaken David to his guilt. We read the account in 2 Samuel 12:1–7:

> Then the LORD sent Nathan to David. And he came to him, and said to him: "There were two men in one city, one rich and the other poor. The rich man had

exceedingly many flocks and herds. But the poor man had nothing, except one little ewe lamb which he had bought and nourished; and it grew up together with him and with his children. It ate of his own food and drank from his own cup and lay in his bosom; and it was like a daughter to him. And a traveler came to the rich man, who refused to take from his own flock and from his own herd to prepare one for the wayfaring man who had come to him; but he took the poor man's lamb and prepared it for the man who had come to him."

So David's anger was greatly aroused against the man, and he said to Nathan, "As the LORD lives, the man who has done this shall surely die! And he shall restore fourfold for the lamb, because he did this thing and because he had no pity."

Then Nathan said to David, "You are the man! Thus says the LORD God of Israel: 'I anointed you king over Israel, and I delivered you from the hand of Saul.'"

David was grief-stricken at this unmasking, this indictment. Verse 13 says, "So David said to Nathan, 'I have sinned against the LORD.' And Nathan said to David, 'The LORD also has put away your sin; you shall not die.'"

With this mighty fall from grace and obedience, David

was stricken by the convicting power of the Holy Spirit. His repentance was as deep as his fall had been steep. His remorse went beyond a superficial fear of punishment to authentic repentance, a spirit marked by a heart broken for offending God. In this attitude of contrition, David penned the prayer known to us as Psalm 51. In this psalm, all the elements of true repentance are found:

> Have mercy upon me, O God,
> According to Your lovingkindness;
> According to the multitude of Your tender mercies,
> Blot out my transgressions.
> Wash me thoroughly from my iniquity,
> And cleanse me from my sin.
>
> For I acknowledge my transgressions,
> And my sin is always before me.
> Against You, You only, have I sinned,
> And done this evil in Your sight—
> That You may be found just when You speak,
> And blameless when You judge. . . .
>
> Purge me with hyssop, and I shall be clean;
> Wash me, and I shall be whiter than snow.
> Make me hear joy and gladness,

That the bones You have broken may rejoice.
Hide Your face from my sins,
And blot out all my iniquities.

Create in me a clean heart, O God,
And renew a steadfast spirit within me.
Do not cast me away from Your presence,
And do not take Your Holy Spirit from me.

Restore to me the joy of Your salvation,
And uphold me by Your generous Spirit. . . .

Deliver me from the guilt of bloodshed, O God,
The God of my salvation,
And my tongue shall sing aloud of Your righteousness.
O Lord, open my lips,
And my mouth shall show forth Your praise.
For You do not desire sacrifice, or else I would give it;
You do not delight in burnt offering.
The sacrifices of God are a broken spirit,
A broken and a contrite heart—
These, O God, You will not despise. . . .

There is a long road between Psalms 1 and 51. This jour-
ney is measured not by pages in a book nor years of personal

experience but between obedience and disobedience, a path well traveled by every Christian. Psalm 1 says:

Blessed is the man
Who walks not in the counsel of the ungodly,
    Nor stands in the path of sinners,
    Nor sits in the seat of the scornful;
But his delight is in the law of the LORD,
    And in His law he meditates day and night.
He shall be like a tree
    Planted by the rivers of water,
    That brings forth its fruit in its season,
    Whose leaf also shall not wither;
And whatever he does shall prosper.

The ungodly are not so,
But are like the chaff which the wind drives away.
Therefore the ungodly shall not stand in the judgment,
Nor sinners in the congregation of the righteous.

For the LORD knows the way of the righteous,
But the way of the ungodly shall perish.

At one point in his life David could be described as the embodiment of the man in Psalm 1, a man like a tree planted by rivers of water. He had meditated on God's Word day and night. In this fire David's spiritual strength had been forged. But somewhere along the way his attention was diverted from that Word to a woman, Bathsheba. As a result, he became like the chaff the wind drives away. In his mighty fall, David lost not only his integrity, but his joy as well.

In Psalm 51, David begs God to cleanse him of his sin, crying: "Make me hear joy and gladness, that the bones You have broken may rejoice. . . . Restore to me the joy of Your salvation."

Though sin brings great pleasure, it brings no joy. If we understand the difference, we can avoid the pitfalls that entice the believer. In his grief David longed to experience afresh the joy of his salvation.

The time of greatest joy in my life was my conversion to Christ, the defining moment of my whole life. Compared to that, nothing else in the world seemed of any value.

I hear that testimony often. My friend John Guest, a British preacher and evangelist, tells of the night he was converted in Liverpool, England. He says that he didn't merely run home, he actually skipped, leaping over fire hydrants along the way. My wife, Vesta, kept waking up during the night following her conversion, pinching herself and asking, "Do I still have it?" Satisfied that she did still have it, she would fall back asleep.

As a new Christian I was infatuated with Scripture. I wanted to spend almost every waking moment reading it. In my first semester of college I made the dean's list. It was not the list of academic achievement, however; it was the list of students placed on academic probation. I made A's in gym and in Bible, and all the rest D's. The A in Bible kept me from flunking out of school.

During those initial months of my Christian life, I was given to tremendous mood swings, from tremendous spiritual highs to frightful lows. I visited a minister, seeking counsel. He explained that such a spiritual roller-coaster ride was not uncommon in new Christians, and that as I matured in my faith my ups and downs would even out. He also counseled me to look to the Bible and not my feelings as the basis of the Christian life. I've never received wiser counsel.

THE WORD IN CONVERSION

God is pleased to use Scripture to pierce the heart and awaken us to faith. Faith does indeed come from hearing and hearing from the Word of God. Hebrews 4:12–13 says:

For the word of God is living and powerful, and sharper than any two-edged sword, piercing even to the division of soul and spirit, and of joints and marrow, and is a discerner of the thoughts and intents of the heart. And there is no creature hidden from His sight, but all things are naked and open to the eyes of Him to whom we must give account.

History is replete with stories of how great people were converted through the power of the Word. Augustine, living a life of sheer immorality, one day heard children playing a game in which they shouted the refrain, "*Tolle Lege, Tolle Lege,*" Latin for "Take up and read." As he heard this, his eyes fell upon the open text of a Bible where he read, "Let us walk properly, as in the day, not in revelry and drunkenness, not in lewdness and lust, not in strife and envy. But put on the Lord Jesus Christ, and make no provision for the flesh, to fulfill its lusts" (Romans 13:13–14).

When Augustine read the words ". . . not in revelry and drunkenness, not in lewdness and lust . . . ," he was pierced by the Word of God and made alive by the Spirit of God.

Centuries later, Martin Luther was awakened in similar fashion. Luther had struggled deeply with the justice of God, admitting that at times he hated the very concept.

Then, while reading Augustine's commentary on Romans 1:17, Luther suddenly saw the truth of the gospel, that the righteousness of Christ is given by faith alone. This awakening in Luther launched the Protestant Reformation.

Romans was also instrumental in the conversion of John Wesley. He was at Aldersgate in London when he heard a sermon preached from Romans and felt his heart "strangely warmed." Wesley considered that the moment of his conversion.

My own conversion was also precipitated by the piercing power of Scripture. I was talking with an upperclassman my first week of college. He was the first person I had ever met who spoke of a personal relationship with Jesus. We had a general conversation, with no formal presentation of the gospel, but he spoke of the transcendent wisdom of the Bible. He cited a somewhat obscure passage from Ecclesiastes: "And if a tree falls to the south or the north, in the place where the tree falls, there it shall lie" (11:3*b*). The words of that text hit me right between the eyes. Suddenly I envisioned myself as the tree, immobile, lying there and simply rotting away. Like the decaying tree I saw my life full of corruption, slowly decaying. With that in my mind I went to my room and was driven to my knees. I knelt beside my bed and begged God to forgive me of my sins. In that moment I met Christ, who gave me a new life and lifted my rotten soul from the floor of the forest. I think it is probable that in the entire history of the Christian church I am the only person to have been converted by that verse in Ecclesiastes.

THE WORD IN SPIRITUAL GROWTH

Just as the Word of God is used in our conversion, so it is a critical instrument in our spiritual growth. By immersing ourselves in the Word of God, we begin to gain the mind of Christ and learn what discipleship is.

Facing death, the apostle Paul wrote his final letter to his dear friend and disciple Timothy. Paul's charge was a call to a diligent study of Scripture: "But you must continue in the things which you have learned and been assured of, knowing from whom you have learned them, and that from childhood you have known the Holy Scriptures, which are able to make you wise for salvation through faith which is in Christ Jesus" (2 Timothy 3:14–15).

The first time I read that passage, I noticed how close it was to Paul's declaration in 4:7, "I have fought the good fight, I have finished the race, I have kept the faith." It was as though the words were haunted. I had heard them before but did not know they were from the Bible. When I was a teenager my father was stricken with severe strokes. For two years all he could do was sit in a chair with a magnifying glass, reading his Bible. It was my job to drag him, fireman style, to the dining room table each night for dinner. One evening as I took him back to his chair he asked me to stop and let him sit on the living room sofa. As he sat he looked at me and said, "Son, I have fought the good fight, I have finished the race, I have kept the faith." This was the first time I ever heard these words, and I had no idea they were from Scripture. But I knew what he meant, and I didn't like it at all. I answered brusquely, "Don't say that, Dad."

I took him to his chair in the den without speaking further. About an hour later I heard a crash in the den. I found my father on the floor with blood seeping from his ears and nose. He was in a coma from which he did not awake. It turned out that the words Paul wrote to Timothy were the last words my father spoke on this earth.

It is clear to me that this exhortation to continue in the Scripture was vital to Paul's own ability to fight the fight, run the race, and keep the faith. By continuing to study the Bible we grow in faith and are able to live the Christian life. In his exhortation to Timothy, Paul directed his disciple to the Scriptures, commending them to him because of their nature and function. He wrote: "All Scripture is given by inspiration of God, and is profitable for doctrine, for reproof, for correction, for instruction in righteousness" (2 Timothy 3:16).

The source of Scripture is God. That Scripture is "given by inspiration" refers not to the way God oversaw the writing of the Bible but to the source of the content of the Bible. The word that is translated "given by inspiration" is the Greek term *theopneust*—literally, "God-breathed." When Paul wrote that Scripture is *God-breathed,* the idea is not one of *inspiration* but of *expiration;* that is, the Bible is *breathed out* by God. The whole point here is that the Bible comes from God. It is His word and carries with it His authority.

As a student and a scholar I have been taught to always check the source of any statement. Credibility is directly tied to source. Reporters sometimes cite "unimpeachable sources" for their information. The only *truly* unimpeachable source is God. Paul wants Timothy to understand the *source* of the Bible, not the *way* it was inspired.

After stating that the Bible is God-breathed, Paul spells out its purpose and value. The Scripture is said to be *profitable* for several things, including *doctrine, reproof, correction,* and *instruction in righteousness.* The value of the Bible is first that it teaches sound doctrine. Though we live in a time when sound teaching is denigrated, the Bible places a high value on it. Much of the New Testament is concerned with doctrine. The teaching ministry is given to the church for building up its people. Paul says, "And He Himself gave some to be apostles, some prophets, some evangelists, and some pastors and teachers, for the equipping of the saints for the work of ministry, for the edifying of the body of Christ" (Ephesians 4:11–12).

The Bible is also profitable for reproof and correction, which we as Christians continually need. It is fashionable in some academic circles to exercise scholarly criticism of the Bible. In so doing, scholars place themselves above the Bible and seek to correct it. If indeed the Bible is the Word of God, nothing could be more arrogant. It is *God* who corrects *us;* we don't correct Him. We do not stand over God but under Him.

This yields a practical help for Bible study: *Read the Bible with a red pen in hand.* I suggest that you put a question mark in the margin beside every passage that is unclear or hard to understand. Likewise, put an *X* beside every passage that offends you or makes you uncomfortable. Afterward you can focus on the areas you struggle with, especially the texts marked with an *X.* This can be a guide to holiness, as the *X*'s show us quickly where our thinking is out of line with the mind of Christ. If I don't like something I read in Scripture, perhaps I simply don't understand it. If so, studying it again may help. If, in fact, I do understand the passage and still don't like it, this is not an indication there is something wrong with the Bible. It's an indication that something is wrong with *me* that needs to change. Often, before we can get it right in any endeavor, we need to first discover what we're doing wrong.

When Christians experience the "changing of the mind" that is *repentance*, we are not suddenly cleansed of all wrong thinking. The renewing of our minds is a lifelong process. We can accelerate this process by focusing on those passages of Scripture that we don't like. This is part of the "instruction in righteousness" of which Paul speaks. The goal of this instruction is that God's people may be complete and equipped for good works.

GETTING STARTED

You've no doubt heard this cliché: "The road to hell is paved with good intentions." Virtually every Christian at some point has resolved to read the entire Bible. If we believe the Bible is the Word of God, it's natural not to want to miss a word of it. If God delivered a letter to your mailbox, I am sure you would read it. But the Bible is a pretty big letter, and its sheer bulk is somewhat daunting, even to the person with the best of intentions.

At seminars I often ask for a show of hands indicating how many people have read the entire Bible. Rarely do even 50 percent of the people raise their hands. I ask, "How many of you have read the Book of Genesis?" Almost everyone raises his hand. Then I say, "Keep your hand up if you've also read Exodus." Only a few hands are lowered. "Leviticus?" Now hands start dropping quickly. With Numbers it's even worse.

Reading Genesis is almost like reading a novel. It is mostly narrative history and biography. It contains important events in the lives of important people like Noah, Abraham, Jacob, and Joseph. Exodus is likewise gripping, as it tells the poignant story of Israel's slavery in Egypt and of their liberation under the leadership of Moses. The contest with Pharaoh is exciting. When we get to Leviticus, everything changes. It's difficult reading about the ceremonies, the rituals of sacrifice and cleansing, and so forth that are foreign to us today. We lack a road map to help us through these difficult portions.

When I enrolled in college, I declared myself a history major. That lasted one semester. My first course was the

History of Civilization, which covered the scope of history from the ancient Sumerians up to the Eisenhower administration. I was quickly lost and confused by the sheer amount of data I tried to assimilate. It was a clear case of information overload. I had no framework in which to process the dates, persons, events, and other facts that assaulted my memory bank. I was grateful for the D that I received for the course and hurried to change my major to something else.

What happened to me in this history class is what happens to many Christians who try to read the Bible from cover to cover. I think there is a better way to go about it. For Christians to truly understand the Bible, they need first to gain an understanding of its basic structure and framework.

The New Testament calls us to a life of discipleship. The word *disciple* means "learner." In any discipline, it is important to begin with the fundamentals and master them. Arnold Palmer once remarked that only about one in fifty amateur golfers holds the club with a proper grip. Legendary coach Vince Lombardi, when agitated by the sloppy play of his team, always called them back to the fundamentals. He would stand before them with a football in his grasp, hold it up for the whole team to see and say, "This is a football. [pause] Am I going too fast?"

Sometimes we chafe at learning the basics. Recently I

began to take violin lessons. My teacher is a highly skilled and accomplished Russian violinist. She worked with me for weeks on how to hold the bow before she would let me actually put the bow on the strings. During that time I learned more Russian than I did violin. The word *nyet* is now a regular part of my vocabulary. I wanted to run before I learned how to walk.

To be sure, the Scripture calls us to maturity. We are not to be satisfied with milk but are to desire the meat of the Word. Hebrews 5:12–14*a* says:

> For though by this time you ought to be teachers, you need someone to teach you again the first principles of the oracles of God; and you have come to need milk and not solid food. For everyone who partakes only of milk is unskilled in the word of righteousness, for he is a babe. But solid food belongs to those who are of full age.

I think that one of the reasons many Christians never get to the meat of the Word but remain at the milk level is because they never really learned how to drink the milk. There is a reason why scales are important to the piano player and the grip to the golfer. We must master these basics if we are to reach higher levels of proficiency.

Begin with an overview of the Bible. Get the basic framework first. If possible, enroll in a class that provides such an overview. We at Ligonier Ministries have produced an audio and video series entitled *Dust to Glory*. It gives the basic structure of the Bible from Genesis to Revelation. It does not go into details but covers the high points of redemptive history. In addition to this series, I collaborated with Robert Wolgemuth to produce *What's in the Bible?* The goal of this book is to help the person who has never had a simple introduction to the Bible. In 1977 I published a book entitled *Knowing Scripture,* which is designed to help people master the basic rules of biblical interpretation. In addition, here is a suggested reading pattern for people who have never read the Bible:

- Genesis (history of the Creation, the Fall, and the covenantal history of the Patriarchs)
- Exodus (history of Israel's liberation and formation as a nation)
- Joshua (history of the military conquest of the Promised Land)
- Judges (transition from tribal federation to monarchy)
- 1 Samuel (emerging monarchy with Saul and David)
- 2 Samuel (David's reign)

- 1 Kings (Solomon and the divided kingdom)
- 2 Kings (the fall of Israel)
- Ezra (the return from exile)
- Nehemiah (restoration of Jerusalem)
- Amos and Hosea (examples of Minor Prophets)
- Jeremiah (example of a Major Prophet)
- Ecclesiastes (Wisdom Literature)
- Psalms and Proverbs (Hebrew poetry)

The New Testament overview includes:

- Gospel of Luke (life of Jesus)
- Acts (the early church)
- Ephesians (introduction to the teaching of Paul)
- 1 Corinthians (life in the church)
- 1 Peter (introduction to Peter)
- 1 Timothy (introduction to the Pastoral Epistles)
- Hebrews (Christology)
- Romans (Paul's theology)

In reading this list, the student gets a basic feel for and understanding of the scope of the Bible. From there he or she can fill in the gaps to complete the reading of the entire Bible.

As a practical matter you may want to combine your reading of the Old and New Testaments. It may help to read a certain number of chapters in the Old Testament and then read some in the New until the study is completed. Martin Luther recommended that his students read through the whole Bible every year to keep the winds of the whole blowing through their minds while concentrating on a particular portion of the Bible.

IMPORTANT TOOLS

I highly recommend using a study Bible. My preference is *The New Reformation Study Bible*. A good concordance will help you find particular verses and add insight into the meaning of important concepts. Audiotapes of the Bible can be used while driving or at other times.

Bible study is one of the most enriching experiences a Christian can have. Faith begins and is strengthened in the Word, for here we encounter the very mind of God.

2

PRAYER

In a small town in Germany a barber went to his shop early one morning. His name was Peter Beskindorf, better known in the village simply as "Master Peter." This morning he was busy shaving one of his regular customers when a large man entered his shop. Peter recognized the man immediately as a fugitive who was wanted by the authorities. Indeed, there was a price on the man's head, but Peter said nothing about that. When Master Peter finished with his client, the big man sat down in the barber chair and asked him for a shave and a haircut.

Peter accommodated the visitor's request and began stropping his razor and preparing the lather for his face. He began the shave, pressing the sharp edge of the blade against the man's neck. Peter knew that with the slightest pressure he could slit the man's throat and collect the bounty.

But Peter had no intention of carrying out such a grisly deed. He knew the man. This was not the first time he had visited his shop or sat in his chair. Indeed, he not only knew the man but loved him as well. More than a customer, the man was Peter's friend, his mentor, and his hero. The man in Peter Beskindorf's barber chair in the village of Wittenberg, Germany, was Martin Luther.

On this day, while shaving Martin Luther, Master Peter said to the great reformer, "Dr. Luther, would you be willing to teach me how to pray?" Luther replied that he would be delighted to help. In fact, the very busy doctor of theology, leader of the Protestant Reformation, retired to his quarters and penned a booklet especially for Peter entitled *A Simple Way to Pray*.

Luther's booklet focused on *how* to pray. But first let's address the question *"Why pray?"*

WHY SHOULD WE PRAY?

Of the many legitimate answers to this question, we will focus particularly on three: first, because prayer is a *duty* for every Christian; second, because prayer is a *privilege;* and third, because prayer is a powerful *means of grace.*

PRAYER AS A DUTY

The Bible makes it abundantly clear that God's people are called to be people of prayer. The Old Testament contains numerous examples of men and women who prayed fervently. We think, for example, of Hannah, who begged the Lord for a son:

Then Elkanah her husband said to her, "Hannah, why do you weep? Why do you not eat? And why is your heart grieved? Am I not better to you than ten sons?"

So Hannah arose after they had finished eating and drinking in Shiloh. Now Eli the priest was sitting on the seat by the doorpost of the tabernacle of the LORD. And she was in bitterness of soul, and prayed to the LORD and wept in anguish. Then she made a vow and said, "O LORD of hosts, if You will indeed look on the affliction of Your maidservant and remember me, and not forget Your maidservant, but will give Your maidservant a male child, then I will give him to the LORD all the days of his life, and no razor shall come upon his head."

And it happened, as she continued praying before

the LORD, that Eli watched her mouth. Now Hannah spoke in her heart; only her lips moved, but her voice was not heard. Therefore Eli thought she was drunk. So Eli said to her, "How long will you be drunk? Put your wine away from you!"

But Hannah answered and said, "No, my lord, I am a woman of sorrowful spirit. I have drunk neither wine nor intoxicating drink, but have poured out my soul before the LORD. Do not consider your maidservant a wicked woman, for out of the abundance of my complaint and grief I have spoken until now."

Then Eli answered and said, "Go in peace, and the God of Israel grant your petition which you have asked of Him."

And she said, "Let your maidservant find favor in your sight." So the woman went her way and ate, and her face was no longer sad. (1 Samuel 1:8–18)

After God answered Hannah's prayer she prayed again, this time a prayer of thanksgiving. It bears a remarkable similarity to the prayer of Mary, the mother of Jesus, in her Magnificat. (Compare 1 Samuel 2:1–10 with Luke 1:46–55.)

Hannah's prayer is but a single example of a multitude of prayers recorded in the Old Testament. The Psalms contain an entire collection of prayers by David and others. The New Testament also bears witness to the regular custom of prayer among believers and even—*especially*—by Jesus Himself. Since prayer is characteristic of our biblical forebears, it serves as a normative standard for us as well.

Beyond these examples, we have the explicit commands given to us by the apostles and by Jesus. The apostle Paul frequently urges his readers to be diligent in their prayer lives. For example, he says:

> . . . rejoicing in hope, patient in tribulation, continuing steadfastly in prayer. (Romans 12:12)

> Do not deprive one another except with consent for a time, that you may give yourselves to fasting and prayer; and come together again so that Satan does not tempt you because of your lack of self-control. (1 Corinthians 7:5)

> Be anxious for nothing, but in everything by prayer and supplication, with thanksgiving, let your requests be made known to God. (Philippians 4:6)

> . . . for it is sanctified by the word of God and prayer. (1 Timothy 4:5)

Jesus tells us to always pray and not give up. In the parable of the unjust judge He says:

> Then He spoke a parable to them, that men always ought to pray and not lose heart, saying: "There was in a certain city a judge who did not fear God nor regard man. Now there was a widow in that city; and she came to him, saying, 'Get justice for me from my adversary.' And he would not for a while; but afterward he said within himself, 'Though I do not fear God nor regard man, yet because this widow troubles me I will avenge her, lest by her continual coming she weary me.'"
>
> Then the Lord said, "Hear what the unjust judge said." (Luke 18:1–6)

In this parable our Lord speaks of something that we "ought" to do (namely, always to pray). The word *ought* describes an ethical or moral necessity. Whatever Jesus says we "ought" to do becomes a solemn duty for us to perform.

PRAYER AS A PRIVILEGE

The obligation or duty of prayer is balanced by its being a privilege as well. When Paul speaks of the fruits and consequences of our justification he writes: "Therefore, having been justified by faith, we have peace with God through our Lord Jesus Christ, through whom also we have access by faith into this grace in which we stand, and rejoice in hope of the glory of God" (Romans 5:1–2).

In the Old Testament, "access" to God was limited by virtue of the separation between the holy place of the Temple and the holy of holies. Of course believers could pray, but they were kept a certain distance from the glorious presence of God. Only the high priest, one day out of the year, was permitted to enter the holy of holies. A thick curtain called the wall of separation guarded the entrance. But when Jesus was crucified, an earthquake struck Jerusalem, and in its upheaval that curtain was torn open. By the atoning death of Christ we are now given a new, freer kind of access to the Father. Christ has won for us peace with God and the end of estrangement. We are now invited by our prayers to enter into the holy of holies. What a great privilege!

As we enter, we come now not as strangers or aliens but as privileged children, adopted into the family of God. The family metaphor is intensified in the New Testament, where the church is metaphorically called the bride of Christ.

Consider Paul's teaching in 2 Corinthians 11:1–2: "Oh, that you would bear with me in a little folly—and indeed you do bear with me. For I am jealous for you with godly jealousy. For I have betrothed you to one husband, that I may present you as a chaste virgin to Christ."

We struggle with the use of the term "jealousy" in the Bible because we tend to think of jealousy as a sin, a sin linked to envy and covetousness, traits unbecoming to the Christian. Yet the Scriptures describe God as a "jealous" God. When the Bible speaks in this manner, it is not expressing the sentiment that God is somehow green with envy toward His creatures as though we possessed something that He lacked. He is not jealous *of* us; He is jealous *for* us. That is, God is vitally concerned for our well-being. This is what Paul means by "godly jealousy." Paul is jealous for the well-being of his spiritual children because of their betrothal to Christ.

Paul takes the marriage metaphor even further in Ephesians 5:22–33. This text is controversial in our day because it calls for the submissiveness of the wife to the husband. That matter aside, the text probes into the mystical relationship between Christ and His bride, the church. This relationship has been related historically to what the Apostles' Creed calls the "Communion of Saints."

Christianity is not an exercise in mysticism. The usual goal of mystical religions is to reach spiritual unity with God. The desire is often expressed in terms of being "one with the universe" (or some other object). The goal is for the individual's identity to merge with the whole, like a drop of water that falls *into* the ocean and eventually can no longer be distinguished *from* the ocean.

Such mysticism is radically different from Christianity. The Christian faith never sees our goal as *becoming* God or as losing our individual identity by being *swallowed up in* God. The goal of spiritual growth is not the kind of union with God that destroys our personalities. Instead, it is a special spiritual union in which rich *communion* takes place.

Prayer and spiritual communion are linked this way: the word *communion* is composed of the prefix "com," which means simply "with" and the root word *union*. In communion we experience a union such as that experienced in marriage, which offers the closest possible level of relationship between two people. The Bible speaks of marriage as an experience wherein the two become one. In this kind of unity, the two persons do not lose their individual identities. Rather, they experience a level of interaction that brings a spiritual unity to the bond.

The New Testament frequently says that in conversion, by the work of the Holy Spirit, we are made to be "in Christ." We are also taught that Christ *indwells* His people so that every Christian is "in Christ," and Christ is "in" every Christian.

In the New Testament, which was originally written in

Greek, a language shift occurs that is not apparent in an English translation. When the Bible calls us to *believe in Christ,* the word for *in* is the Greek word *eis.* Literally this term means "into." If you were outside a room and wanted to be inside, you would have to move through a door or some other means of access to get there. This transition is a moving *into.* Once the transition has been made, you are no longer outside the room but inside of it. The Greek word for this is *en.*

In New Testament terms, we are "in Christ" because by faith we have moved into Him and He has moved into us. It is the most glorious marriage of all, the marriage that results from the soul's union with Christ.

Our union with Christ is the basis for our union with each other. If I am in Christ and He is in me, and you are also in Christ and He is in you, then obviously we are both united to Christ. All who are united to Christ are also united to each other. This is why the church is referred to as the mystical body of Christ and the communion of the saints.

As wonderful as this communion of saints is, it is not worthy to be compared to communion with Christ. This communion with Him is the foundation for our *communication* with Him in prayer.

People with marriage troubles frequently experience a breakdown in communications. A wife may say, "My husband doesn't talk to me." When communication fails, the basic communion between two persons fails with it.

Marriages don't usually begin that way. Couples usually communicate well during the courtship period. My wife and I dated for more than eight years before we got married. During six of those years we went to different schools. I called her long-distance every day and wrote her a letter every night. She also wrote me every day. We desired to stay in close communication with each other. I didn't make those calls or write the letters out of duty but out of desire. Our letters weren't newsletters; they were love letters. That's what prayer is: communication of those who have a love relationship with Christ. What a privilege we have.

PRAYER AS A MEANS OF GRACE

We pray not only because it is our duty and our privilege, but also because prayer is a powerful means of grace. That is, God uses prayer to bring His will to pass.

Does prayer change things? We must answer with a resounding, "Yes." Prayer changes *us* and prayer changes *things*. James 5:13–18 teaches us:

> Is anyone among you suffering? Let him pray. Is anyone cheerful? Let him sing psalms. Is anyone among

you sick? Let him call for the elders of the church, and let them pray over him, anointing him with oil in the name of the Lord. And the prayer of faith will save the sick, and the Lord will raise him up. And if he has committed sins, he will be forgiven. Confess your trespasses to one another, and pray for one another, that you may be healed. The effective, fervent prayer of a righteous man avails much. Elijah was a man with a nature like ours, and he prayed earnestly that it would not rain; and it did not rain on the land for three years and six months. And he prayed again, and the heavens gave rain, and the earth produced its fruit.

This passage teaches that "the fervent prayer of a righteous man avails much." To "avail much" means *to make a significant impact.* This prayer is *effective.* It has *real power.*

The power of prayer is a *means* that God uses to bring about His intended *ends.* Just as God uses the preaching of the gospel as the power unto salvation, so likewise He uses the power of prayer to bring about redemption. Our prayers cannot force God to do anything, but He uses them as His own instruments to bring about His will.

Monica was the mother of Saint Augustine. Monica was a devout Christian woman, and she grieved deeply over her wayward son who as a young man was unconverted and unbridled in his sin. Monica prayed with tears every day for his conversion. On one occasion she visited her pastor, the famous bishop Ambrose of Milan, looking for comfort and some assurance that her prayers were not in vain. Ambrose sought to comfort her with a rhetorical question, "Monica, could a child of so many tears possibly be lost?"

The answer Ambrose intended to his question was, "No." He assumed that any child whose mother prayed for him so faithfully would surely eventually come into a state of grace. I disagree. The tearful prayers of a grieving mother do not guarantee her child's conversion. The probability of it is high, however, at least high enough to take great comfort in it. I may preach with passion and tears, yet no one is converted. But I know that in the final analysis God's Word will not return to Him void, and in like manner the prayers of His people are never wasted. Prayer works, and that is a tremendous incentive to pray.

HOW SHOULD WE PRAY?

We remember that Master Peter's request of Martin Luther was not to teach him *why* he should pray but *how* he should pray. This is a most important issue. So often, pastors and teachers exhort congregations to act a certain way because it is their duty, but then they fail to teach how to do it.

The *how* question is what motivated the disciples to ask Jesus to teach them to pray. Obviously they had noticed a link between the extraordinary power of Jesus and His prayer life. Jesus answered their request by providing them, and us, with what we call the Lord's Prayer:

Now it came to pass, as He was praying in a certain place, when He ceased, that one of His disciples said to Him, "Lord, teach us to pray, as John also taught his disciples."

So He said to them, "When you pray, say:

Our Father in heaven,
Hallowed be Your name.
Your kingdom come.
Your will be done
On earth as it is in heaven.
Give us day by day our daily bread.
And forgive us our sins,
For we also forgive everyone who is indebted to us.
And do not lead us into temptation,
But deliver us from the evil one." (Luke 11:1–4)

A PRAYER MODEL

The Lord's Prayer is a model. It gives us not only an actual prayer to pray but also a pattern to follow in prayer. Consider the first phrase, for example. The prayer begins with a personal form of address in which God is called "Father." This was a radical thing in Jesus' day because Jews did not address God as "Father." Not only did Jesus constantly call Him "Father," He invites us to do the same.

The first petition is that the name of God be regarded as holy. From there Jesus moves to a request for the kingdom of God to triumph. We are to pray for that kingdom to come and the will of God to be done on earth as it already is done in heaven.

I've often wondered if there is a logical link between the first petition of the Lord's Prayer and the next two. If so, it means that until the name of God is regarded as holy, we cannot expect to see His kingdom come or His will done on the earth as it is in heaven, where God is surrounded by the seraphim who continually sing, "Holy, holy, holy."

So we need to begin our prayers by bowing in reverence before our God, acknowledging Him as our loving and holy heavenly Father.

A KINGDOM FOCUS

Just as the Lord's Prayer emphasizes the kingdom of God and His glory, so should our prayers. This means praying beyond our own circumstances and needs—seeing the bigger picture and praying for God's work in the rest of the world.

Recently, Archie Parrish led a seminar in our church during which he organized us into "Fire Teams." These are groups of four people who meet regularly to encourage each other in the discipline of prayer. For the first three months, the groups agree to pray each day for fifteen minutes. In the second three months the daily prayer time is extended to thirty minutes. Every three months the time is increased fifteen minutes until the prayer warriors are praying for sixty minutes a day. We now have more than sixty people in our congregation doing this.

In addition, the congregation as a whole has pledged to pray for my family and me at every meal. It is an extraordinary blessing for me, as it would be for any minister, to be upheld by so much prayer from the congregation. I believe a praying church will always be an effective church.

PRACTICAL SUGGESTIONS

As a practical guide for this prayer enterprise, Archie published a little booklet wherein he comments on Luther's

A Simple Way to Pray. More than anything else I've ever encountered, this little book has changed the way I pray. Luther suggested to Master Peter that he set aside time for prayer every day. Because pressures frequently threaten to disrupt our prayer time, it is helpful to have a regular time or times scheduled. Luther also suggested that, like Jesus, Master Peter get apart to a quiet place where it is easier to concentrate. Luther told him, "Prayer is like your task as a barber. The last thing I want you to do is to have your mind wandering when you've lathered up my face and you take out that blade and start shaving me. I don't want you to start woolgathering and end up slitting my throat."

Perhaps the richest suggestion I gleaned from Luther's booklet is to pray "through" three things: the Lord's Prayer, the Ten Commandments, and the Apostles' Creed. There is an important difference between *praying* the Lord's Prayer, for example, and *praying through* the Lord's Prayer. To pray through the Lord's Prayer is to focus attention on each of the petitions for a time. For example, instead of simply praying, "Hallowed be Thy name," I might say, "O Lord, we live in an age where Your name is not only not revered or honored but is used as profanity. Bring such an awakening to Your glory that no one would think of dragging Your name through the mud or treating it as common or trivial.

Let it be on our lips and in our hearts as an expression of our adoration for You. Give me grace to always respect Your sacred name in my heart and with my lips."

In similar fashion we continue to pray for those things set forth in the Lord's Prayer, the Ten Commandments, and the Apostles' Creed. We pray that we will not slip into any form of idolatry by placing other gods before Him. In the Creed we exalt the majesty of the One who is the "Maker of heaven and earth." These three items give us "pegs" to hang our prayers on.

People often balk at the idea of spending a full hour in prayer. The point is not to be rigid in timing our prayers or guilt-ridden if we fail. Luther said that there were times when the cares of the day were so pressing on him that he simply put his head on his pillow at the end of the day and prayed the Lord's Prayer, recited the Ten Commandments and the Creed, then fell asleep.

Another simple way to structure prayer is using the acrostic *ACTS*. The letters stand for: *Adoration, Confession, Thanksgiving,* and *Supplication.* I use this structure for pastoral prayers in church. It keeps us focused on the vital elements that every prayer should contain. So often our prayers are limited to personal appeals for whatever blessings we would like to receive from God, or requests for our friends and relatives. We learn this at an early age when we pray, "God bless Mommy, Daddy, sister, brother, Grandma . . . ," etc. Of course it is good to pray for family, friends, and those in need. But we need to understand that prayer is more than supplication and intercession.

I confess I am really surprised by Jesus' answer to the disciples' request that He teach them how to pray. I would have expected Him to say something like, "If you want to master the art of prayer, immerse yourself in the Psalms—prayers that were inspired by the Holy Spirit." Or He might have directed them to the recorded prayers of saints such as Hannah or Nehemiah. Instead, He gave them a model for communicating with God that has inspired, comforted, and strengthened Christians for two thousand years.

Whether we use as our model the Lord's Prayer, the Ten Commandments, the Apostles' Creed, *ACTS,* or something else altogether, the important thing is that *we pray*. Personally, I will be forever grateful to that barber in Wittenberg for daring to ask Dr. Martin Luther to teach him how to pray. Thanks to his request and Luther's simple answer, multitudes have dug deeper into the life of prayer.

3

WORSHIP

The father of the two boys was bursting with pride. It is one thing to have a son follow in your footsteps, quite another to have two. The father was a minister, and he was watching now the ordination of his sons to that same ministry.

The young ministers were zealous for their work. They decided to experiment, to add something new to the worship service. What happened was far from what they expected. Not only did God disapprove of their innovations, He manifested His disapproval by killing them on the spot. This dreadful event is recorded in Leviticus 10:1–3:

> Then Nadab and Abihu, the sons of Aaron, each took his censer and put fire in it, put incense on it, and offered

profane fire before the LORD, which He had not commanded them. So fire went out from the LORD and
devoured them, and they died before the LORD. And Moses
said to Aaron, "This is what the LORD spoke, saying:

'By those who come near Me
I must be regarded as holy;
And before all the people
I must be glorified.'"

So Aaron held his peace.

This grim episode in the history of ancient Israel makes an
unforgettable point: *worship of the living God is serious business.*
It is not something to be trifled with or taken lightly. God is
serious about how we worship Him, and we must be, too.

During the 1920s, Babe Ruth was invited to London to
visit the king of England. As preparation for his audience with
the king, Ruth was instructed in proper court etiquette. He
was told what the protocol should be when he was ushered
into the presence of His Majesty. After all of the coaching and
training, when the moment came, Babe Ruth walked up and
simply said, "Hi, King," almost setting off a diplomatic crisis.

I experienced culture shock when I enrolled in the Free
University of Amsterdam in the Netherlands and went to

my first class with Professor G. C. Berkouwer. Dr. Berkouwer came in from the side door, and immediately every student stood at attention. He walked to the podium, nodded, and the class was seated. He opened his notebook and proceeded to deliver his lecture without interruption. No student dared to raise his hand or ask a question. At the end of his lecture he closed his book and turned toward the door. As he did, the students stood again as he walked out. This was the way people showed respect to the clergy or professors.

I will never forget the embarrassing moment I had one unusually warm day. I was sitting at the back of the amphitheater. It was so hot that I took off my coat. (We always had to wear a coat and tie.) I took off my jacket and set it on the edge of my chair, at which point Dr. Berkouwer stopped in mid-sentence, looked straight at me and said, "Would the American please put his coat back on?" He did not yet know me, but he knew I had to be an American. Only an American would have dared insult him by taking off his coat in the presence of the professor.

This is something we need to be alert to in our culture. We have proclaimed our independence from monarchs and have little respect for sovereignty. We don't know much about paying homage. We don't know the "proper court etiquette," particularly when we come into the presence of our King.

IN SPIRIT AND IN TRUTH

Again we remember Jesus' discussion with the woman at the well at Sychar, when they discussed where God was to be worshiped (John 4). Jesus said the time has come and now is when God is to be worshiped *in spirit and in truth*. When Jesus says the true worshiper is to worship God in Spirit and in truth, He is obviously drawing a distinction between *true* worship and *false* worship.

The woman is concerned with the *where* of worship, but Jesus says God is omnipresent, and so therefore we can worship God anywhere. The problem Jesus is addressing here is that sometimes people show up *physically* to worship, but they're not into it *spiritually* at all. Jesus says God is pleased with people who worship Him with their hearts fully engaged and who delight in honoring God with sincere, heartfelt worship.

The psalmist says, "I was glad when they said to me, 'Let us go into the house of the LORD'" (Psalm 122:1). Spiritual worship is offered by the person who takes delight in honoring God, in praying to God, in listening to God with his or her mind fully engaged in the Word of God.

Worship that is pleasing and acceptable to God is worship that is offered in *truth*. We live in an age that downplays the importance of truth, emphasizing fellowship and emotional experience. Truth means getting at who God really is, and God is most fully revealed in Jesus, who said, "I am the truth" (see John 14:6). How can someone say he loves God but doesn't care about truth? I hear people say, "Doctrine divides." Of course doctrine divides, but it also unites. It unites the ones who love truth, who love God's truth, who are willing to worship Him according to the truth. God wants people to worship Him from the heart and from a mind that is informed of who He is by His Word.

Throughout Scripture we are commanded by God to come into His presence—to come near to *Him*. That's why we worship. It is an unbelievable privilege. It is also the very first consequence of our justification. According to Romans 5:1–2: "Therefore, having been justified by faith, we have peace with God through our Lord Jesus Christ, through whom also we have access by faith into this grace in which we stand, and rejoice in hope of the glory of God."

Now every Christian is allowed to come into God's very presence. There is no more a wall of separation. It's not just the high priest who can go, one day a year, after elaborate ritual cleansing. All believers are now invited to come into the immediate presence of God. We don't have to be priests to do it. And not only that, Hebrews 4:16 says that we may come *boldly* into His presence.

But there is a difference between coming *boldly* into the presence of God and coming *arrogantly*. When we come boldly into His presence and draw near to Him, we must always remember that we are to regard Him as holy. Jesus spoke to His disciples about His current generation, "These people draw near to Me with their lips, but their hearts are far from Me." What Jesus was saying is that when we draw near and regard Him as holy, that regard, that homage, can't be just from our lips. It's got to be from the *heart*.

PREPARATION

Let us remember the awesome circumstances of the giving of the Law in Exodus 19. God called the people to prepare to come into His presence, or *near* His presence, but not actually onto the mountain where He would speak to Moses. Exodus 19:10 says, "Then the LORD said to Moses, 'Go to the people and consecrate them today and tomorrow, and let them wash their clothes.'" He said: I want those people, before they come near Me, to *get ready* to come near Me, to *prepare* to come near Me.

Our church service begins at 10:30 A.M. At 10:20 we turn down the lights and the prelude begins. This is our signal to get ready to worship. God gave Israel two days to get ready, to prepare. He required them to wash their clothes, to get ready for the third day. "For on the third day the LORD will come down upon Mount Sinai in the sight of all the people" (Exodus 19:11*b*). This is an extravagant announcement. If I told my congregation that in three days God was going to appear visibly, and they knew it would happen, and that God wanted them to wash their clothes for the occasion, I am sure they would do it.

> For on the third day the LORD will come down upon Mount Sinai in the sight of all the people. You shall set bounds for the people all around, saying, "Take heed to yourselves that you do not go up to the mountain or touch its base. Whoever touches the mountain shall surely be put to death. Not a hand shall touch him, but he shall surely be stoned or shot with an arrow; whether man or beast, he shall not live." When the trumpet sounds long, they shall come near the mountain.
>
> So Moses went down from the mountain to the people and sanctified the people and they washed their clothes. (19:11*b*–14)

Then, in verse 16 we read:

> Then it came to pass on the third day, in the morning, that there were thunderings and lightnings, and a thick cloud on the mountain; and the sound of the trumpet

was very loud, so that all the people who were in the camp trembled.

When the trumpet sounded and the moment arrived to draw near, every person in the camp trembled. Unfortunately, that's not how some people worship anymore. Many have forgotten how to tremble before Him, have not regarded Him as being holy. Verses 17–22 continue:

And Moses brought the people out of the camp to meet with God, and they stood at the foot of the mountain. Now Mount Sinai was completely in smoke, because the LORD descended upon it in fire. Its smoke ascended like the smoke of a furnace, and the whole mountain quaked greatly. . . .

And the LORD said to Moses, "Go down and warn the people, lest they break through to gaze at the LORD, and many of them perish. Also let the priests who come near the LORD consecrate themselves, lest the LORD break out against them."

Over and over again God invites the people, "Come on . . . come near . . . *But I will be regarded as holy by those who come near to Me.* Let the priests come, but only after they have been consecrated, only after they have prepared themselves to come into My presence."

Finally, let's look at similar instructions that we find in the New Testament, in Hebrews 10:19: "Therefore, brethren, having boldness to enter the Holiest"—not just the holy place, but the *holy of holies*—"having boldness to enter the Holiest by the blood of Jesus, by a new and living way which He consecrated for us, through the veil." Here the veil that consecrated the access to God was not the veil that hung in the Temple. The veil that hung in the Temple was that which concealed the glory of God from human sight. But on the day of Christ's crucifixion, the veil of the Temple was torn, and the veil *now* was the flesh of Christ that hid His divine glory—that glory which broke through on the Mount of Transfiguration when Jesus' glory could not be contained within His flesh. That's what Peter meant when he said, "[We] were eyewitnesses of His majesty . . . when we were with Him on the holy mountain" (2 Peter 1:16*b*, 18*b*).

"He consecrated for us, through the veil, that is, His flesh, and having a High Priest over the house of God, let us draw near" (Hebrews 10:20*b*–22*a*). In Israel, the work of the high priest made it possible for the people to be cleansed and to approach the place of meeting in the Tabernacle and later in the Temple. But now we have a High Priest who goes not simply into the earthly Tabernacle but who has entered into the heavenly Tabernacle. He goes into the very presence of the Father, on our behalf, as our Mediator, as our High Priest. And because we have this—our own High Priest over the House of God—"let us draw near with a true heart in full assurance of faith, having our hearts sprinkled from an evil conscience and our bodies washed with pure water" (10:22).

Nobody wants to come near to God with an uneasy conscience. Sin is one of the reasons why we like to keep a safe distance from Him. It goes back to the Garden of Eden. After that very first transgression, when God came into the Garden, the last thing Adam and Eve wanted was to experience His nearness. Instead of rushing to Him, to greet Him and embrace Him as they had before, they ran for the woods. They ran for cover, trying to avoid the nearness of God.

But here the New Testament tells us to come near with a firm faith, with full assurance *because our consciences are clean*. If we haven't been keeping short accounts with God, however, we will not be comfortable coming near to Him. This is something every Christian experiences.

But we have had "our hearts sprinkled from an evil conscience and our bodies washed with pure water. Let us hold fast the confession of our hope without wavering, for He who promised is faithful" (Hebrews 10:22b–23). We read the law and the law convicts us. But the law also points to the Gospel. Though it's simple to understand the Gospel in our heads, to *really believe* that we are made right with God by the righteousness of Christ *alone* is not as easy. He covers us with the cloak of His righteousness, so that *our sin* is covered by *His perfection*. That's what makes it possible for us to come into the presence of God. Otherwise, God wouldn't want to even look at us.

ASSEMBLING

Hebrews 10:24–25 continues: "And let us consider one another in order to stir up love and good works"—*listen*—"not forsaking the assembling of ourselves together, as is the manner of some. . . ." Some Christians do neglect that solemn assembly, the gathering together of the saints. Surveys tell us that in the most vibrant churches in the United States on any given Sunday at least 25 percent of the congregation is absent. Part of that is because of illness, part because of vacations or being out of town. But also it happens because people sometimes just don't feel like coming.

If we don't feel like going to church, we are to do it anyway. It's a privilege to come near to God and to worship with other believers, but it's also a most sacred duty. I would be completely derelict in my duty if I didn't tell you that God takes that very, very seriously. And we have this admonition not to neglect our assembling together. So if we get up and don't feel like going to church and want to go to the beach instead, we must say to ourselves, "Wait a minute, if I do this, I'm neglecting the God who has redeemed my soul from the pit. I'm going to church." That will probably be the very day that God showers His grace upon us.

EXHORTING

The passage also says, "exhorting one another, and so much the more as you see the Day approaching" (v. 25*b*).

Exhorting one another, encouraging one another—that is the clear admonition of Scripture. Again, these are two sides of the same coin—*Come near,* God says. Come near to Me, and I will draw near to you.

> Seek the LORD while He may be found,
> Call upon Him while He is near.
> Let the wicked forsake his way,
> And the unrighteous man his thoughts;
> Let him return to the LORD,
> And He will have mercy on him;
> And to our God,
> For He will abundantly pardon. (Isaiah 55:6–7)

When we come to church on Sunday morning, we enjoy fellowship with one another. We benefit from the encouragement we get from being with friends who are praying for us, who are also on a spiritual pilgrimage. In the New Testament, fellowship was an important part of the Sunday experience of Christians. But the *primary* reason to be in church is to worship the living God, and for this we must bring a sense of reverence and adoration for His transcendent majesty. There's nothing common about this. We walk through that door. We step across the threshold. We enter into His presence. We know that God is not restricted to this building but that this is a sacred hour that God has set apart and declared to be a holy time of visitation between Himself and His people. We come now into His magnificent presence. We leave worldly cares and concerns for a while and focus on God. The pulpit is not a place for pop psychology. The pulpit is a place where the Word of God is to be proclaimed—not the opinions of the pastor. People come to hear a word from God. It is the pastor's responsibility to make sure what they hear from the pulpit *is* the Word of God. That's where the power is. That's where the truth is. That's what we all desperately need to hear, and more than once a week. And so we come to hear and respond in a way that will honor God, in a way that will honor His majesty—that people will sense that they are in the presence of the holy.

GLORIFY

The principle that transcends the ages is that what we do on Sunday morning must add to the sense of the unsurpassed majesty of God. "And before all the people I must be glorified" (Leviticus 10:3*b*). The word *glory* in the Old Testament is the Hebrew word *kabod*. Its roots mean literally "that which is heavy" or "that which is weighty." "Kabod" refers to God's heaviness or weightiness—His transcendent and eternal dignity, which commands instantaneous respect and homage from every creature. No one should come into the presence of the God of glory in a flippant and cavalier manner. If we really understand who God is and that we're in His presence, we will be on our faces before Him, giving Him the honor and the magnificence that He deserves.

Here we're talking about the sovereign God of the universe, before whom the nations tremble. If we do not learn to honor Him now, we will certainly tremble before Him later. The lesson of Nadab and Abihu should drive us to serious and careful reflection about how we worship God.

God wants people who worship Him from the heart, and from a mind that is informed of who He is by His Word. Worship that honors God must be in Spirit and in truth.

4

SERVICE

She is ninety-eight years old—pushing hard against the century mark. For years my mother-in-law has regaled our family with rich tales of life on a Midwestern farm before automobiles, airplanes, indoor plumbing, and electricity. Her stories, spun with a beaming face and glistening eyes, mesmerize my grandchildren with life that seems to them to be from another planet. Sleighs pulled by the family horse, visits to the privy in the dead of night, no television, radio, or computers.

But the stories have stopped. The face is now pale and somber. The gleam has left her eyes. Multiple mini-strokes and one major stroke have left her a mere shadow of her former self. She's still "Grandma," but her life is now managed by caregivers who attend to her twenty-four hours a day. She lives in our home. She still sits with us at the table but cannot feed herself. Her words are mostly incoherent.

It is sad to watch her weaken daily. Yet it is a study in grace to watch the tender care she receives from her caregivers. Two of them listen to my radio program, *Renewing the Mind*. Both of these women are absolutely delightful. They told me their Christian faith had an impact on their work, because caregiving is a real ministry. As I watched them give day-to-day attention to the detailed needs of my mother-in-law, I realized I was watching a model of biblical service in action.

The five actions we are exploring in this book are all *means of grace*. A means of grace is a tool or instrument that God uses to strengthen and nurture us as we grow in conformity to Christ. We don't always think about service as a means of grace, but we *grow* as we *serve*. The more we are able to serve in the kingdom of God, the more Christlike we become. So it is with the caregivers. I could see what it was doing for their Christian growth to be in a profession that is a service ministry. All believers are called to be servants of God—not necessarily *professional* servants or *paid* servants, but each of us is to be involved in some kind of service to God and to His people. One of the ways we serve God is by serving people. That theme is woven throughout Scripture.

Think for a minute of one of the primary examples of

this in the Old Testament, the Exodus. The story of the Exodus begins with the people of Israel in servitude to a foreign master.

> Now there arose a new king over Egypt, who did not know Joseph. And he said to his people, "Look, the people of the children of Israel are more and mightier than we; come, let us deal shrewdly with them, lest they multiply, and it happen, in the event of war, that they also join our enemies and fight against us, and so go up out of the land." Therefore they set taskmasters over them to afflict them with their burdens. And they built for Pharaoh supply cities, Pithom and Raamses. But the more they afflicted them, the more they multiplied and grew. And they were in dread of the children of Israel. So the Egyptians made the children of Israel serve with rigor. And they made their lives bitter with hard bondage—in mortar, in brick, and in all manner of service in the field. All their service in which they made them serve was with rigor. (Exodus 1:8–14)

We are told that when God appears to Moses, He says, "I have heard the cries of My people, and I want you now to go to Pharaoh, and you tell Pharaoh that I said to let My people go."

This story has great irony. The redeeming action of God begins when He hears the cries of His people groaning under the burden of their bondage to the harsh taskmaster, the pharaoh of Egypt.

God did more than merely listen to their cries, however; He took action to free them from Pharaoh. He appeared to Moses in the burning bush, calling him to confront Pharaoh and lead the children of Israel out of Egypt. Notice carefully what God said:

> And the LORD said: "I have surely seen the oppression of My people who are in Egypt, and have heard their cry because of their taskmasters, for I know their sorrows. So I have come down to deliver them out of the hand of the Egyptians, and to bring them up from that land to a good and large land, to a land flowing with milk and honey, to the place of the Canaanites and the Hittites and the Amorites and the Perizzites and the Hivites and the Jebusites. Now therefore, behold, the cry of the children of Israel has come to Me, and I have also seen the oppression with which the Egyptians oppress them. Come now, therefore, and I will send you to Pharaoh that you may bring My people, the children of Israel, out of Egypt."

But Moses said to God, "Who am I that I should go

to Pharaoh, and that I should bring the children of Israel out of Egypt?" (Exodus 3:7–11)

The irony is this: we see what God redeems His people *from,* but don't miss what God redeems them *to.* He calls His people out of Egypt, out of slavery, not to become autonomous or do whatever they please. He calls them out of Egypt that they might *serve God:*

> So He said, "I will certainly be with you. And this shall be a sign to you that I have sent you: When you have brought the people out of Egypt, you shall serve God on this mountain." (Exodus 3:12)

The Israelites were called *out of* service to Pharaoh, *into* service to God. In a very real sense, the Exodus in the Old Testament functions as an image to prepare us for the ultimate exodus that is accomplished in the New Testament through our Deliverer, Jesus. Christ comes not to take us out of Egypt but to free us from bondage to Satan. Yet, when Christ delivers us out of this bondage, we experience an exchange of masters. Now He calls us to be *His* servants. There is a sense in which we have to be servants. The only issue is, of whom? Jesus Himself said, "You cannot serve two masters" (see Matthew 6:24). We can serve Satan, we can serve the interests of this world, or we can serve the living God and be servants of Christ. It's extraordinary that Paul's favorite description of himself is as a *doulos,* or a slave—one bought with a price—and he says to us that we are not our own, but we have been "bought at a price" (1 Corinthians 6:20). We belong to the One who has paid for us, who has redeemed us, and now we are called to serve Him.

This idea of service is deeply rooted in the Old Testament. We see it in the moving story of what took place in Shechem toward the end of Joshua's life. He assembled the people to renew their oath to the covenant they had made with God. Joshua 24:14 says, "Now therefore, fear the LORD, serve Him in sincerity and in truth, and put away the gods which your fathers served on the other side of the River and in Egypt. Serve the LORD!" He gave the people this mandate: "You've been serving the wrong things—the Canaanite deities, the pagan idols. Put those away and serve the Lord," he says, "in sincerity and in truth."

Does that strike a chord? Remember Jesus' teaching to the woman of Sychar (John 4)? We read that God is seeking those who will worship Him in Spirit and in truth. What Jesus says to the Samaritan woman, Joshua says here to all of the people assembled: "Serve [the Lord] in sincerity and in truth." And then he goes on to say, "If it seems evil to you to serve the LORD"—if you don't want to serve the Lord—"choose for yourselves this day whom you will serve, whether the gods which your fathers served that were on the other side of the River, or the gods of the Amorites, in whose land you dwell. But as for me and my house, we will serve the LORD." That should be the commitment and motto of every Christian. "As for me and as for my house, we're going to serve the Lord with single-minded devotion."

Service, however, is not high on our list of things to enjoy. In our culture, we struggle with the image and role of the servant. We think it's beneath our dignity.

Many years ago when I was in seminary, I had a revelation about my own feelings about servitude. One summer vacation, I got a job in the maintenance department of a large hospital in Pittsburgh. One of my jobs was to sweep the parking lots every morning, cleaning up the cigarette butts and refuse left from the night before. I cleaned the parking lots and the streets in front of the hospital as well as the parking lot of the dormitory for nursing students.

When I was in high school, there was a clearly defined "pecking order" of graduates. At the top was the "elite" group who went away to college. The next rung on the ladder was the group who enrolled in nurses' training. Since I had graduated college and was now in graduate school, I was in the academic *crème de la crème*. But during the summer I was literally pushing a broom. When the student nurses exited their dorm, I greeted them. My epiphany came when they tilted their caps up in the air and walked past me as though I were invisible. It was beneath their dignity to talk to me because I was a lowly servant, sweeping the parking lot. I'll never forget that experience. I wanted to say, "Wait! You don't understand. I'm a college graduate. You are just in nurses' school. You don't understand the pecking order here." I didn't like being treated like a servant. I remember wrestling with that afterward and thinking, *You're supposed to be a Christian, and here you were upset because someone regarded you as a servant.* Yet Jesus Himself said, "I didn't come here to be served; I came to serve" (see Matthew 20:28). And He passed that legacy on to all of His people.

Jesus' disciples also struggled with servanthood:

But Jesus called them to Himself and said, "You know that the rulers of the Gentiles lord it over them, and those who are great exercise authority over them. Yet it shall not be so among you; but whoever desires to become great among you, let him be your servant. And whoever desires to be first among you, let him be your slave—just as the

Son of Man did not come to be served, but to serve, and
to give His life a ransom for many." (Matthew 20:25–28)

The disciples didn't understand Jesus' definition of
greatness. So He said to them, "Whoever desires to become
great among you, let him be your servant." This mandate
was not just given to twelve people. It was for the whole
kingdom of God. It is the law of the King that we are to
imitate Him by being servants.

In the New Testament, a particular burden was placed
upon the apostles that cost them their lives. They were
commanded of Christ to go into the world and preach the
gospel. And that was their mission—to the Jew first, then
to the Gentile. Yet for the church to fulfill this preaching
mission, a host of menial tasks had to be cared for such as
the serving of tables.

Now in those days, when the number of the disciples
was multiplying, there arose a complaint against the
Hebrews by the Hellenists, because their widows were
neglected in the daily distribution. Then the twelve sum-
moned the multitude of the disciples and said, "It is not
desirable that we should leave the word of God and serve
tables. Therefore, brethren, seek out from among you

seven men of good reputation, full of the Holy Spirit and wisdom, whom we may appoint over this business; but we will give ourselves continually to prayer and to the ministry of the word."

And the saying pleased the whole multitude. (Acts 6:1–5*a*)

Every believer is called to ministry. We're called to see that all of the tasks of the kingdom take place—that the poor are ministered to, the gospel is proclaimed, the Word of God is taught, and worship takes place. But that doesn't mean that everyone is called to be an evangelist, or a preacher, or a teacher. The New Testament teaches that God gives every Christian a gift to be used for the service of Christ. If your gift is teaching, then you had better teach; if it's preaching, you'd better preach; if it's evangelism, you'd better evangelize. If your role is to be a caregiver to shut-ins, then be a caregiver to shut-ins. But each one of us is called to do our part, thus ensuring that all the ministry is fulfilled.

Luke 17 records the disciples' coming to Jesus and asking Him for a raise. Not a raise in pay, however; what they wanted elevated was their faith. They obviously saw a link between their Lord's faith and His power. Note how Jesus responds to their request:

And the apostles said to the Lord, "Increase our faith."

So the Lord said, "If you have faith as a mustard seed, you can say to this mulberry tree, 'Be pulled up by the roots and be planted in the sea,' and it would obey you. And which of you, having a servant plowing or tending sheep, will say to him when he has come in from the field, 'Come at once and sit down to eat'? But will he not rather say to him, 'Prepare something for my supper, and gird yourself and serve me till I have eaten and drunk, and afterward you will eat and drink'? Does he thank that servant because he did the things that were commanded him? I think not. So likewise you, when you have done all those things which you are commanded, say, 'We are unprofitable servants. We have done what was our duty to do.'" (Luke 17:5–10)

What an odd way for Jesus to answer their request. He tells them this story about servants coming in from completing their tasks in the field. And Jesus says, "Does the master of the servants say, 'Oh, you've done such a great job. Sit down, eat, drink, enjoy yourselves'? Or does he say, 'Now it's time for you to fix my meal. You set the table. You serve me, and when all your tasks are done, then you can go eat and drink'?" Jesus is teaching here about servanthood. Perhaps the single most important truth we can learn about this is that we, who are His servants, are *unprofitable* servants.

When Jesus says that we are unprofitable servants, He does not mean that our service is of no value. Jesus frequently called His disciples to be productive. When He says we are unprofitable servants He means we gain no "bonus points" or merit from our service. Jesus says that's not possible (Luke 17). What deed could I possibly do that was not what God required of me in the first place? Remember, He commands us to be perfect, and we can't improve on perfection. We can't even hope to reach that goal.

I have no "profit" of my own because I earn nothing by doing what I am required to do in the first place. That's why our redemption is by *grace* and grace *alone*. The only thing that I have to place before God that is, properly speaking, my own, is my sin. The only thing that can redeem me is not *my* works, but the work that *Christ has performed in my behalf.* He freely came to do the Father's will and to submit Himself to the Law for our sake. He, and He alone, is a profitable servant.

If we serve trying to earn our way into the kingdom of God, we're deceiving ourselves. The motivation for Christian service is *gratitude*, not earning salvation. Service is a means of grace, of realizing our dependence on grace and growing in that grace. My friend John Piper has awakened people to a concept of vital importance to our Christian faith—the *joy* in rendering obedience to God. John says that the motive for our obedience should *not* be simply an abstract sense of duty. (I believe sometimes we do have to obey out of duty, which is better than disobedience. There are times when we don't enjoy the prospect of obedience, and we can't just wait until we feel like doing it.) He's right: it should be our delight to obey God, motivated by joy for what He has done for us, not out of grim obligation or as a means to gain heaven.

We are "unprofitable servants" in this world. In heaven, however, this same Christ, who says all we are doing is what we are commanded to do, tells us that God will reward His people *according to their works*. We must be careful with that phrase "according to." That does not mean that our works *earn* the reward. But God in His grace will distribute rewards according to our service—even though our works don't deserve it. This is a gracious distribution of rewards, or as Saint Augustine said, "God crowning His own gifts."

In Luke 19:12–27, Jesus gives us more important teaching about servanthood:

Therefore He said: "A certain nobleman went into a far country to receive for himself a kingdom and to return. So he called ten of his servants, delivered to them ten minas, and said to them, 'Do business till I come.' But his citizens hated him, and sent a delegation after him, saying, 'We will not have this man to reign over us.'

"And so it was that when he returned, having received the kingdom, he then commanded these servants, to whom he had given the money, to be called to him, that he might know how much every man had gained by trading. Then came the first, saying, 'Master, your mina has earned ten minas.' And he said to him, 'Well done, good servant; because you were faithful in a very little, have authority over ten cities.' And the second came, saying, 'Master, your mina has earned five minas.' Likewise he said to him, 'You also be over five cities.'

"Then another came, saying, 'Master, here is your mina, which I have kept put away in a handkerchief. For I feared you, because you are an austere man. You collect what you did not deposit, and reap what you did not sow.' And he said to him, 'Out of your own mouth I will judge you, you wicked servant. You knew that I was an austere man, collecting what I did not deposit and reaping what I did not sow. Why then did you not put my money in the bank, that at my coming I might have collected it with interest?'

"And he said to those who stood by, 'Take the mina from him, and give it to him who has ten minas.' (But they said to him, 'Master, he has ten minas.') 'For I say to you, that to everyone who has will be given; and from him who does not have, even what he has will be taken away from him. But bring here those enemies of mine, who did not want me to reign over them, and slay them before me.'"

This is a parable of capitalism, a parable of productivity. Jesus is saying with respect to stewardship, as well as service, that His people are called to delay their gratification. We are called to invest in the future so that our investments may grow. He tells this story of the rich master who has to go away, just as Jesus has ascended into heaven and left us behind with the treasures that we have during His absence. And what is He saying? "When I come back, I expect to find that that which I have given you has gained in value, that progress is made because My people have been productive servants." We may be "unprofitable," but that doesn't mean we're to be *unproductive*. "Let's sleep in tomorrow, hide our gifts, so that when He comes back, we can say, 'Here are the gifts You gave us. Nothing happened to them.

They're just as good as when You left.'" Jesus says, "I'll take that away from you and give it to the man who multiplied his gifts ten times, who used the gifts I gave him for the sake of the kingdom."

This is a heavy parable of service. It reveals that one of the worst things we can do is to waste the gifts that God has given us. Those gifts are given to us for Christ's sake, for His glory, and for His honor. He's the One before whom all the inhabitants of heaven cast down their golden crowns beside the glassy sea (Revelation 4:6, 10). They take their gifts and present them to Christ because they are His in the first place. And that is what we are to do with our service. We are to be productive servants.

The apostle Paul amplifies our responsibilities as servants in 1 Corinthians 4:1–2: "Let a man so consider us, as servants of Christ and stewards of the mysteries of God. Moreover it is required in stewards that one be found faithful."

A steward in the ancient world was someone who was given the responsibility to manage the household. That person was entrusted with the possessions of the owner. The chief requirement of the steward was fidelity. An unfaithful steward was a crook, somebody who would steal from the owner. And Paul is saying, "Do you realize that we are servants, and stewards of the mysteries of God? God has entrusted these things to us."

> But with me it is a very small thing that I should be judged by you or by a human court. In fact, I do not even judge myself. For I know of nothing against myself, yet I am not justified by this; but He who judges me is the Lord. Therefore judge nothing before the time, until the Lord comes, who will both bring to light the hidden things of darkness and reveal the counsels of the hearts. Then each one's praise will come from God. (1 Corinthians 4:3–5)

"My stewardship, my service," Paul says, "is not to be judged by men." The value of my stewardship will be judged by Christ and not by human beings—not by you, not even by myself because I can't give an accurate assessment of my own service and obedience. None of us can read anyone else's heart. Only the searcher of human hearts can do that. That's why the service that we are to give is to be unto the Lord and before His scrutiny.

Our servanthood should require no supervision, no need to have someone looking over our shoulders to ensure that we are working. Our task is to please *Christ,* not perform merely for the applause of people. People-pleasers cannot be true servants of Christ.

With the eyes of the world on the firemen, policemen, and rescue workers standing in the rubble of what once was the World Trade Center in downtown Manhattan, we have seen models of selfless service. The firefighters who lost their lives rushing to rescue those trapped in the World Trade Center on September 11, 2001, were not people-pleasers. Their service was authentic.

A few blocks from Ground Zero in New York City is the meeting place for Redeemer Presbyterian Church, one of the brightest models of a serving church to be found anywhere. This church, under the leadership of its pastor, Timothy Keller, has taken the biblical concept of service and put skin and bones on it. They are pioneers in mercy ministry.

For Christians who want practical direction for how to serve, I strongly recommend that they not merely read, but *study* Tim Keller's little book, *Resources for Deacons*. It is the best manual for service training I've ever seen. It's published by the Presbyterian Church in America.

Christian service is not limited to Presbyterians or times of great crisis. It is a sacred call to every Christian.

5

STEWARDSHIP

It was 1947. I was so excited—I was about to see my first major-league baseball game. My uncle held my hand as we walked up the ramp toward our seats at Forbes Field. From our vantage point I could see players practicing on the grass. I could see the ivy-covered walls, the old iron gate behind the monument in center field, and the high screen guarding the right-field stands where Babe Ruth had hit his last home run.

Suddenly my uncle stopped. He said to me, "Hold on to your wallet!" I immediately did so. When we took our seats I asked, "Can I let go of my wallet now?" My uncle said, "Yes." When I asked him why he had told me to do that he said, "See that man over there with the turned-around collar? He's a priest. You always have to hold on to your wallet when a priest or a minister comes near. They're all out to get your money."

My first baseball game (Pirates 5, Cincinnati 2) was also my first exposure to a cynical attitude toward tithing and charitable giving.

My father did not share my uncle's cynicism. He preached tithing to us as children. Every week I was required to put 10 percent of my allowance in the offering plate at church. I was introduced to this practice long before I was a Christian.

A widespread cynicism toward giving remains in our culture. Some unscrupulous televangelists have given tithing a bad name. Yet the Bible commands Christians to be good stewards.

We take an offering every Sunday in our church. Right before the offering, I usually say, "Let us now worship God with our tithes and offerings." The point I'm stressing to our congregation is that giving should be an act of worship.

THE TITHE IN THE OLD TESTAMENT

The Bible's first recorded offering is found in Genesis 4, brought by the brothers Cain and Abel:

> And in the process of time it came to pass that Cain brought an offering of the fruit of the ground to the LORD.

Abel also brought of the firstborn of his flock and of their fat. And the LORD respected Abel and his offering, but He did not respect Cain and his offering. And Cain was very angry, and his countenance fell. (vv. 4:3–5)

Why was Abel's offering more pleasing than Cain's? Some think it was because Abel's offering was an animal—a blood sacrifice—while Cain's was merely from the fruit of the ground. Yet throughout the Old Testament God made provisions for such sacrifices that were fully acceptable to Him. Cain offered his kind of sacrifice because he was a tiller of the ground, while Abel was a shepherd. The text doesn't indicate that being a shepherd was somehow holier than being a farmer.

Hebrews 11:4 provides the key: "By faith Abel offered to God a more excellent sacrifice than Cain, through which he obtained witness that he was righteous, God testifying of his gifts; and through it he being dead still speaks."

It seems then that what pleased God was the manner in which Abel gave his offering: he gave it *in faith*. Presumably Cain did not. Indeed, his faithlessness was soon manifested in his jealous rage against his brother.

We remember from our earlier look at worship that God seeks those who will worship Him in Spirit and in truth. Abel did. Abel offered to God the sacrifice of praise by making his offering in faith. This is the very essence of worship.

The idea of sacrifice goes to the very heart of biblical faith. Foreshadowing the perfect redemptive work of Christ, Old Testament worship focused on the sacrificial system. When someone entered the Old Testament Tabernacle, the first article of furniture he saw was the altar of burnt offering.

Christian churches today feature no such altars of burnt offering. The days of blood sacrifices and animal sacrifices are over. The perfect, once-for-all sacrifice of Christ has taken away that need.

> For Christ has not entered the holy places made with hands, which are copies of the true, but into heaven itself, now to appear in the presence of God for us; not that He should offer Himself often, as the high priest enters the Most Holy Place every year with blood of another—He then would have had to suffer often since the foundation of the world; but now, once at the end of the ages, He has appeared to put away sin by the sacrifice of Himself. And as it is appointed for men to die once, but after this the judgment, so Christ was offered once to bear the sins of many. To those who eagerly wait for Him He will appear a second time, apart from sin, for salvation.

For the law, having a shadow of the good things to come, and not the very image of the things, can never with these same sacrifices, which they offer continually year by year, make those who approach perfect. For then would they not have ceased to be offered? For the worshipers, once purified, would have had no more consciousness of sins. But in those sacrifices there *is* a reminder of sins every year. (Hebrews 9:24–10:3, emphasis added)

The atonement of Jesus as our Great High Priest ended the Old Testament sacrificial system, but it did not destroy the principle of sacrifice in the Christian life. We are still called to worship God and to give offerings to Him in that worship. Paul writes in Romans:

I beseech you therefore, brethren, by the mercies of God, that you present your bodies a living sacrifice, holy, acceptable to God, which is your reasonable service. And do not be conformed to this world, but be transformed by the renewing of your mind, that you may prove what is that good and acceptable and perfect will of God. (Romans 12:1–2)

We are to give ourselves to God as *living sacrifices*. We give our time, our energy, and our very selves to Him as acts of worship and gratitude. Biblical giving is part of the overall context of stewardship.

The whole concept of stewardship begins with creation. Creation is celebrated not only in Genesis but throughout Scripture, especially in the Psalms, where part of Israel's worship celebrated God's ownership of the whole universe: "The earth is the LORD's, and all its fullness, the world and those who dwell therein" (Psalm 24:1). God is the author of all things, the Creator of all things, and the owner of all things. Whatever God makes, He owns. What *we* own, we own as *stewards* who have been given gifts from God Himself. God has the ultimate ownership of all our "possessions." He has loaned these things to us and expects us to manage them in a way that will honor and glorify Him.

The word that is translated "stewardship" in the Bible is the Greek word *oikonomia*, from which we get our word *economy.* It is two distinct words joined together to create a new word: *oikos*, which comes from the Greek word for *house*, and *nomos,* the Greek word for *law*. Literally, the word that is translated "stewardship" means "house law," or "house rule."

The steward in the ancient culture was not the owner of the house. He was hired by the owner to manage his house affairs. He managed the property and was responsible to allocate the resources of the home. The steward's job was to make sure that the cupboards were filled with food, the money was taken care of, the lawn was tended, and the house was kept in good repair.

Humankind's stewardship began in the Garden of Eden, where God gave Adam and Eve full dominion over the entire creation. Adam and Eve were not given *ownership* of the world; they were given the responsibility of *managing* it. They were to ensure that the garden was tilled and cultivated, and not abused or exploited, and that the goods God provided were neither spoiled nor wasted.

One of my jobs is to be president of Ligonier Ministries. With that comes the responsibility that every chief executive officer bears—the allocation of resources. We look at our ministry. We have a building to take care of; constituents to minister to; personnel, computers, office equipment, and supplies to manage; and we have money. We have a certain amount of time in which to operate our ministry. We cannot be effective if we waste our time, our people, or our money, or if we mismanage our facility and equipment. To do any of that would be bad stewardship. We understand that handling our resources takes wisdom. If we spend them on one thing we cannot spend them on something else.

In our own households we learn that if we spend fifty dollars on clothes, that's fifty dollars we no longer have for anything else. Everyone, even billionaires, functions with limited resources. Every time we use a resource, we make a decision, and that decision reveals what kind of stewards we are. That's where God holds us accountable. He held Adam and Eve accountable for how they took care of that garden. God is interested in how we take care of our ministries, personal lives, homes—every aspect of life. All of these deal with managing and allocating resources.

One of the most gripping stories in the New Testament is Jesus' parable of the prodigal son. This young man had received an inheritance that he did not earn—his father just gave it to him. His problem, however, was that as soon as he received it, instead of trying to build this inheritance or to invest it (as we saw in the parable of the servants), he went far from home and wasted it on wine, women, and song. He ended up living in a pigsty. This young man is known as a "prodigal" because he wasted his father's resources. Worse, he was wasting his life, the very worst sin against stewardship. Each one of us has been placed on this planet by God to glorify, honor, and serve Him with what we produce and how we live. A wasted life is a tragedy. That was the story of the prodigal son, until he received a new life and was brought to his senses.

He went back home to his father's house in repentance,

willing to give up his rights as a son and to be treated as a hired servant. Instead, his father welcomed him home and held a great celebration for his return—a beautiful picture of the grace and mercy of God for prodigals of all kinds.

As Christians, our most valuable possession is the gift of Christ Himself. It is a gift worth far more than silver and gold, far more than other precious stones. But we carry this treasure in earthen vessels, a beautiful metaphor (2 Corinthians 4:7). To think we carry this precious treasure in common clay pots.

At the center of the biblical concept of stewardship is the tithe. We see it instituted as law in the Old Testament, and many wonder if it carries over into New Testament life.

Let us first look at the role of the tithe in the Old Testament. The word *tithe* means "tenth." The basic principle was that every person was to return one-tenth of his increase to the Lord on an annual basis.

The beauty of the tithe is that it precluded class warfare and the politics of envy. It prohibited unequal taxes from being imposed wherein one group of people paid a higher percentage than another. When that happens, then economics becomes politicized, and it creates vested-interest groups where justice is ignored for the sake of power.

In Israel everybody gave the same *percentage* but not the same *amount*. In this structure a person who makes

$10,000 a year returns $1,000 in tithe. The person who makes $1,000,000 per year returns $100,000. The rich person returns far more money, but it is the same percentage as the poor person.

Trouble developed in the Old Testament when the people held out on their tithes. They were not obedient to God's law. We read in Malachi:

"Will a man rob God?
Yet you have robbed Me!
But you say, 'In what way have we robbed You?'
In tithes and offerings.
You are cursed with a curse,
For you have robbed Me,
Even this whole nation.
Bring all the tithes into the storehouse,
That there may be food in My house.
And try Me now in this,"
Says the LORD of hosts,
"If I will not open for you the windows of heaven
And pour out for you such blessing
That there will not be room enough to receive it."
(3:8–10)

A recent poll of people claiming to be evangelical Christians indicated that only 4 percent of them tithe. A similar poll indicated that the average percentage of income "evangelical" Christians give to God's work is less than 2 percent.

This means that if the tithe principle is still in effect and the polls are accurate, then 96 percent of professing evangelical Christians are systematically robbing God. Malachi's teaching indicates that when we fail to tithe we are not merely robbing the church, the clergy, or Christian educators—*we are robbing God Himself.*

If we ask Christians the question raised in Malachi, "Will a man rob God?" they shrink back in horror. People will say, "We would never think of robbing God!" Yet God's verdict on Israel was precisely that. God challenged them to be faithful, giving His own promise that He would open the windows of heaven and pour out blessings upon them.

Why did God institute the tithe in the first place? We remember that He separated an entire tribe, the tribe of Levi, for ministry. The Levites were set apart to take care of the spiritual and educational responsibilities of the nation.

Perhaps God understood market economics wherein the marketplace establishes the "value" of goods and services. In a marketplace economy such as ours, entertainers, athletes, business entrepreneurs, doctors, attorneys, and others rise to the top of the income charts. Their labors are highly valued. The work of teachers and ministers, however, is not.

In America the lowest paid professional group is the clergy. The second-lowest paid group is schoolteachers. These were precisely the two groups that God ensured would be paid by instituting the tithe in Israel.

Our ministers are not to be paid by the state—it is the church's responsibility to do that. And when the church fails to tithe, it is reflected in the compensation of ministers.

I have heard leaders of church boards say they keep their pastors' salaries low in order to keep them humble and reliant upon God. They want to ensure that ministers are truly dedicated to their work and are willing to sacrifice to carry it out.

It is one thing for a person to sacrifice willingly. It is quite another to have that sacrifice imposed upon him or her. When we impose sacrifices on others, we are in fact exploiting them and violating God at the same time.

When we don't tithe, we reduce the ministry of Christ. One of the greatest barriers to expanding the kingdom of Christ in this world is a financial barrier. A fundamental principle is at work here. If we have $100 to work with in ministry, we are limited by that dollar amount. We can waste that money and do only $10 of actual work. But even if we are expert managers and scrupulous stewards, we cannot do $110 of ministry.

Christian ministry depends upon Christian giving. That giving always and everywhere limits the work of ministry.

THE TITHE IN THE NEW TESTAMENT

Some people say that the tithe does not apply to the New Testament. I think it does. We see people continuing to tithe in the New Testament community in one of the earliest non-biblical books that we have in antiquity. The *Didache*—or so-called "Teaching of the Apostles," written either at the end of the first century or early in the second—has a significant portion of it given to this question of supporting the work of the kingdom. The tithe principle is clearly communicated there. In the earliest documents that we have from the Christian church, we see that the primitive Christian community continued the practice of the tithe. Also, there is in the *Didache* a prudential warning given to the Christian, saying, "Let your donation sweat in your hand before you give it." An interesting metaphor, isn't it? *Let your donation sweat in your hand before you give it.* Notice that the injunction is not for your hand to squeeze the money so hard that you never give it. That's not the point. The point is to be very careful, very discerning where you give your donation.

That brings up a controversial question with respect to

financing the kingdom. Again, in Malachi 3:10 God says, "Bring all the tithes into the storehouse, that there may be food in My house." In the Old Testament, the tithe, either in animals or produce, was brought to a central location, the storehouse, which was managed by the Levites. The whole tithe from the whole nation was brought into this single receiving place, and then was distributed by the Levites according to the needs of the people.

Some people believe that means that in the New Testament age there should be a single storehouse where all the tithes go and then are distributed from that storehouse. There are two problems with that. In the first place, in the Old Testament, the people of Israel had a single central sanctuary. When the New Testament church began, churches were established in every town and every city—in Ephesus, in Corinth, in Thessalonica, and so on. No longer was there one central sanctuary. So the idea of bringing tithes into one central storehouse becomes problematic.

Some people believe that the local church is the storehouse, and is, therefore, the only appropriate place for us to give our tithes. But nothing in the New Testament equates the local church with the Old Testament storehouse. If we believe that the local church *is* the storehouse, we would then have to argue that all tithes should go to a central location for each denomination or perhaps even each entire nation. All of your tithes would have to go to a central receiving house, and then be distributed from there. I have never heard a local church favor that. It is simply not biblical to require people to give their entire tithe to their local church. I do believe that the lion's share of it should go to the local church, but I also think that the principle of letting your donation "sweat in your hand before you give it" implies not only discernment but also liberty in giving so that your giving may include a seminary, a Christian college, and other worthy ministries.

The Bible teaches that we are to invest in the kingdom of God. We live in a country that was built on the principle of capitalism, and the fundamental idea of capitalism is this: *delayed gratification*. Instead of taking the money we make and spending it all now, we save it and invest it. This allows our capital to go to work for us, expanding our wealth.

I really believe that the most important investment we can ever make is in the kingdom of God, because it has eternal returns. These returns are not just for us but also for our family, our children, our grandchildren. This generation of Christians must invest in the things of God for the sake of the next generation. This follows Jesus' admonition: "Seek first the kingdom of God and His righteousness, and all these things shall be added to you" (Matthew 6:33).

I want to give a practical comment on tithing. People say, "I'd like to tithe, but I can't afford to." I honestly believe that if you invest in the kingdom of God, you won't lose anything in the final analysis. Tithe from the top, and learn to do that as early as you can in life. If your child gets a dollar allowance, make sure that the first ten cents goes into the collection plate on Sunday, so the child learns the principle early. We know we cannot spend the tax the government takes out of our paycheck. We must live on our "take-home" pay. Our obligation to God takes precedence over our obligation to government. God should get paid first, "from the top." If you want to know how serious you are about investing in God's kingdom, look at your checkbook. It is an objective, concrete record of where your treasure is and where your heart is.

Giving in itself is a grace that God gives. It is one of the important steps to spiritual growth.

Bible reading, prayer, worship, service, and stewardship: these are five key disciplines for a productive Christian life. All five are vital to our spiritual health and the health of Christ's church. If we as Christians will apply ourselves faithfully to them, we can one day say with Paul, "I have fought the good fight, I have finished the race, I have kept the faith" (2 Timothy 4:7).